The Costa Brava

The Empordà, Girona and the Dalí route

The Costa Brava

Text
LLÀTZER MOIX

Photographs
JORDI PUIG

TRIANGLE POSTALS

CONTENTS

- *Coastal towns*

- *Inland towns*

The Costa Brava

The Costa Brava can be simply defined as a coastline of rocks sculpted by the wind and the sea and covered by a carpet of thicket and pines that twist and turn to the caress of the waves. Grey, blue, green and white: these are the colours of a Costa Brava that also includes long smooth sandy beaches. Its personality however, is determined by an endless succession of coves and unexpected spots.

The appearance of the Costa Brava alters with the different seasons of the year, retaining its beauty throughout. A rainy winter afternoon in Cadaqués; a Tramontana storm swirling the Mediterranean in front of Cap de Creus or a morning of sun, shining over the Medes islands, south of Cap Begur or in any corner of this rugged coast that descends towards Blanes. These are unforgettable spectacles – continuous, with no intervals, open to anyone who wishes to contemplate them – with only one actor: nature. The images gathered in this guide constitute a foretaste of the treasure that is made up of the coastline of the coast of Girona, that to a large extent, is still to be discovered.

The Costa Brava

Costa Brava is the name given to the tourist area at the north-eastern extremity of Spain, above the coastline of Girona. Its geographical limits are the border with France in the north, and Blanes in the south (approx. 60 kms. from Barcelona). It embraces the maritime façades of the Alt Empordà, Baix Empordà and La Selva regions.

The Costa Brava was so named at the beginning of the 20th century in view of its steep relief that is characterized by solid stones that extend down to the same Mediterranean shore. There are gentle coves that alternate with beaches of very different sizes.

The natural beauty and the mild Mediterranean climate (the average summer temperature is around 23 degrees centigrade and there is low humidity thanks to the Tramontana wind) made the area into a tourist focal point already in the first decades of the last century. The first tourists were small groups of occasional summer holidaymakers from Spain or from abroad. Then began the building of private residences that resulted in the establishment of a colony of regular visitors. From the beginning of the 1960's, the Costa Brava went through an important process of changes to satisfy growing demand and became one of the most popular holiday destinations in Europe.

As a result of that overcrowding, the Costa Brava today is a classic tourist destination. Lloret or Platja d'Aro are locations that attract hundreds of thousands of visitors every year. Cadaqués is recognized as being one of the most enchanting fishing villages

Tossa de Mar

of the Mediterranean coastline. The nature reserve of the Medes islands, in front of L'Estartit, is highly valued as an underwater paradise by diving enthusiasts from all over the continent. Tossa de Mar has been visited by great artists for a century now. Port de la Selva, the Cap de Creus Nature Reserve, Roses, Empuriabrava, L'Escala, Begur, Tamariu, Llafranc, Calella, Palamós, S'Agaró and Sant Feliu are also, amongst others, well known locations on the Costa Brava. They form part of a sentimental education for various generations of Europeans.

However, in spite of its traditions and long history, the Costa Brava is still an area that holds surprises for visitors who arrive with a willingness to discover its whole; for those who are not content to limit their stay in their resort. Apart from the already mentioned mythical names, the Costa Brava is attractive as a whole and it is worthwhile exploring as much of the territory as possible. Only by exploring this territory (which is usually done on land but which is also excellent by boat) can one adequately gauge the wealth and diversity of the area.

This guide was written with this idea in mind and it underlines the diversity of the Costa Brava. The collection of images gathered is more than eloquent in displaying a succession of enchanting places. It is also limited and token, owing to the wide areas of the region as well as the limited size of this guide. Its visual information is complemented by texts whose aim is to familiarize the reader with the area and to point out man-made attractions built by the inhabitants of the Costa Brava.

Cadaqués

The light announces daybreak in La Fosca →→

Alt Empordà

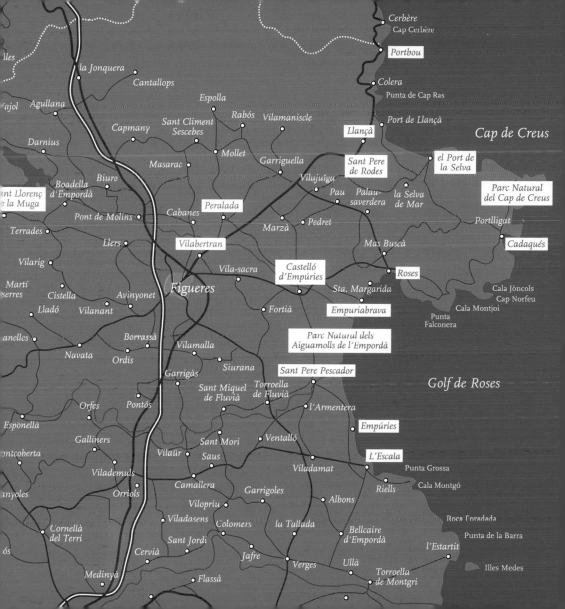

Portbou

The dividing line between France and Spain reaches the Mediterranean sea at the l'Ocell point in Portbou. This is the extreme north of the Costa Brava, the uneven coastline that extends to around a hundred kilometres and ends its extreme south in the locality of Blanes. Portbou is, like Cerbère (the neighbouring French town), a communications knot and a border town in which the train station and the sea are its central elements. The sea here has a brownish tone that occasionally reaches the sands of its beaches. Among these beaches it is worth mentioning Gran and del Claper. Also, towards the south there is Colera, where the 12th century Sant Miguel chapel is worth visiting, as well as the chapels of Barques and Garbet.

Beach of Claper

Portbou, between the sea and the railway

Llançà

Llançà and the harbour of Llançà, originally separate, joined together to form one town as a result of the tourist boom and consequent urban growth. The old centre has the beautiful baroque church of Sant Vicenç. The harbour area, with its modern port facilities that house the moorings for the fishing fleet and recreational boats is located in front of the so called beach of del Port. To the north, beyond the torrent of Valleta, there exist various urbanizations around the beaches of Grifeu, Cap Gras and Canyelles up to Cap Ras point. This point closes Grifeu bay. At the other end, beyond the port, there is the islet of El Castellar which is joined artificially to terra firma. Its high point offers spectacular views of Llançà.

The silhouette of El Castellar caracterizes Port de Llançà

The Port de Llançà beach

El Port de la Selva

El Port de la Selva possesses a splendid bay, a beautiful silhouette of a fishing village, a harbour and a constellation of coves of stunning beauty, on the coast to Cap de Creus. A gentle place, favoured by writers such as Foix and Sagarra, Port de la Selva benefits from being a sheltered location under the protection of the monumental monastery of Sant Pere de Rodes. It is worth visiting the church of Santa Maria de les Neus, the busy terraces of Carrer del Mar and the lighthouse on the S'Arenella point with its stupendous views. Navigating from Cap de Creus to El Golfet (Cala Galera, Talabre, Tavallera...) which is opposite the cove of Portaló, to the old Club Mediterranée, the island and cove of Cullaró, Cala Culip, towards the Claveguera channel, to the S'Encalladora island and Massa d'Or is simply memorable!

The maritime frontage of El Port de la Selva

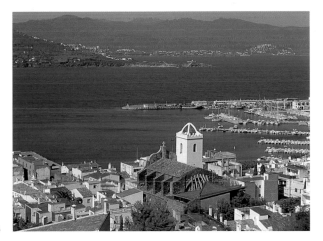

General view of the town

Sant Pere de Rodes

This is a monumental centre whose oldest buildings date from the 10th century. Sant Pere de Rodes is one of the Romanesque jewels of Catalonia. On a mountain elevation and facing the sea, it is irrefutable proof of monastic skill (in this case Benedectine) in building retreats in spots that are very moving. Visitors have to park their vehicles a certain distance away and then walk to the monastery along a path with no parapet, that has a majestic view of the Mediterranean. Within the enclosure, whose restoration includes modern elements, the church stands out. Its nave has beautiful arches, capitals and what has remained of painted murals; it has a Lombard bell tower and cloisters in the abbatial palace. The views from the castle ruins, situated above the monastery, are spectacular. Lovers of architecture can visit the monastery of Sant Quirze de Colera after leaving Sant Pere.

Sant Pere dominates the impressive scenery

Interior of the church

← ↑ Interior and exterior of the bell tower

The view from Sant Salvador →→

Cap de Creus

Seen from the air, the Cap de Creus peninsula appears to be the last swipe taken by the Pyrenees prior to sinking into the sea. This area of rocky terrain, cliffs, small coves and clear waters is often swept by the Tramontana wind. The area has formed part of the Cap de Creus Nature Reserve since 1998. It was the first maritime/terrestrial Nature Reserve in Catalonia and it covers an area of 13,886 hectares, three quarters of which are on land, the rest in the sea. It affects the municipalities of Cadaqués, Port de la Selva, Selva de Mar, Llançà, Vilajuïga, Pau, Palausaverdera and Roses. If it contains treasures on land like Sant Pere de Rodes, it is the sea – from Bol Nou point (Port de la Selva) to Falconera point (Roses) – that boasts ideal places for coastal walks, sailing diving or swimming. In adverse weather conditions it affords the most severe natural spectacles.

*Singular rock formations adorn
Cap de Creus*

The lighthouse, guide for sailors

Cala Guillola, a cove protected from the Tramontana wind
The wind and the sea have carved the Cap de Creus landscape →
The fury of a Levant storm →→

Cadaqués

Cadaqués is probably the town in the Costa Brava that has most successfully preserved its traditional appearance. Located in a wide bay south of Cap de Creus, but separated from the rest of civilization by the El Pení mountain (605m), Cadaqués lived through the first half of the 20th century with a notable autonomy. It was dedicated to looking after its olive groves, fishing and maritime trade. On land, Roses or the neighbouring Port de la Selva seemed far away at the end of an even discouraging path that was full of bends. Legend has it that fishermen from Cadaqués got to know the island of Cuba before getting to know the town of Figueres!

That isolation in an environment of thickets and green and grey slate, burnished by a particularly blinding light, has resulted in being a blessing for Cadaqués. Its white silhouette, with its low buildings crowned by the church of Santa Maria (with its bell tower, its humble rose window and cypresses planted next to its portal), has survived the passage of time. It almost seems to be a framed painting. Behind the façade and criss-crossed by various beaches and coves is a hidden Cadaqués with steep and narrow streets. These have rustic paving and are dotted with benches and flower pots. They are rich in shade, background noises and where time stands still. Without a doubt it was this double factor of picturesque, peaceful village and open fishing village that made Cadaqués a meeting point for artists and intellectuals from all over the planet. At the head of these was Salvador Dalí whose father originated from here. Dalí invited García Lorca and Buñuel, his fellow students in Madrid, to spend the summers in

Regatta of lateen-sail boats

Es Cucurucú crag

Cadaqués. Later he built a shelter in Portlligat bay where he played host to surrealist artists (Paul Eluard, André Breton...). Pablo Picasso, Marcel Duchamp and John Cage were other creative people who lived more or less regularly in Cadaqués.

A result of the attraction that Cadaqués had and still has for artists is the large number of art galleries that exist. This is unusual in a town this size. There are also two museums, the Municipal Museum and the Perrot Moore museum. Furthermore, Cadaqués offers its visitors (that range from the well to do middle class to nomads in the style of Jack Kerouac) an annual international music festival. In spite of these earthly attractions (complemented by a considerable gastronomic offer and a string of bars with a bohemian atmosphere, such as Marítim, Boya, Melitón, Café de La Habana, L'Hostal...). Cadaqués acquires its best dimension from the sea. The bay of Cadaqués, that closes off the Cala Nans lighthouse in the south, is the ideal setting-off point for a boat trip to Cap de Creus.

The constellation of boats present in its waters during a good part of the year bears witness to this. The journey in a northerly direction – whose first obligatory stopover is the bay of Portlligat – is a pure delight. There are a succession of coves that sparkle from the mineral beauty of slate. Jonquet, Guillola, Bona, Jugadora and Fredosa are the names of just some of these shelters on a route that leads to Cap de Creus, dominated by its lighthouse that is exposed to all the winds. The return trip to Cadaqués, illuminated by twilight at the end of the evening, affords an impression of beauty only comparable with the first light of day.

"Steep and narrow streets..."

"...dotted with benches and flower pots"
Baroque altarpiece of the Santa Maria church →
The dawn light gives warmth to the best image of the town →→

Roses

The position of Roses, ending in the gulf that bears its name and protected by Puig Rom (225m) and the Cap de Creus peninsula, has, from a long time, merited worthy consideration. Already in the 4th century B.C. it attracted a Greek colony (Rhode). Later, it housed a Roman colony and then even later, in the era of the county of Empúries it was valued as a strategic enclave. After hundreds of years, emperor Charles V, in the 16th century, ordered the building of a citadel south of the town. The walled ruins can still be seen. Apart from its strategic value, Roses has always been a town with a notable population that in time enjoyed a placid life – like the coastline that flows to the south – as well as an active life as reflected in its position as the main fishing port and its busy tourist activities.

Fishing is an important activity

The bay, with the port in the foreground

Roses also offers archaeological attractions such as the Trinitat castle ruins (next to the lighthouse, above the Poncella point). Towards the interior, further on from the Puig Rom viewpoint, there are the remains of a Visigoth campsite and the dolmen of Creu d'en Corbetella that form part of the biggest megalithic monuments in Catalonia. The journey towards the north coast passes by villas and apartments in the Canyelles Petites and l'Almadrava coves. Further on, buildings are fewer and one reaches desolately beautiful spots like Cap Norfeu, Cala Jóncols and Cala Montjoi where, for six months of the year, the El Bulli restaurant opens. This restaurant, in the last decade, has become a point of pilgrimage for the most famous chefs from all over the world who are attracted by its revolutionary cuisine.

The Canyelles Petites beach

Ruins of the old citadel

The promenade
View of Roses from Santa Margarida →
La Rubina beach →→

Empuriabrava

The passion for sailing that accompanied the growth of the Costa Brava generated a considerable interest in the property market from sailing enthusiasts for a second home with a driveway in the front garden and a boat mooring at the rear. This demand resulted in the building of an extraordinary urbanization within the city limits of Castelló d'Empúries, next to Muga river, where the road joins the boating channels from the marina. Located in the far north of the urbanization, there are two main channels that branch out to create a system that is complemented by some twenty minor channels that partly take advantage of the attributes of a terrain that was originally marshland. Thus, there is a "Venice effect" without giving up traffic on four wheels!

The tower of the yacht club dominates the marina

The urbanization seen from the air

One of the main canals

The building of an aerodrome (that has been a centre for skydiving, light aircraft and ultra-light aircraft flying) boosted the already good Empuriabrava communications and made it especially attractive for people from other countries.

This urbanization also has one of the deepest strips of beach to be found in the Costa Brava, and links the two rocky extremes of the Roses bay in a gentle dip. Beyond this beach there are floodlands that have been successfully cultivated and the Aiguamolls de l'Empordà Nature Reserve, with its impressive bird population.

Further north, the Santa Margarita urbanization reproduced, on a smaller scale, but with a more basic network of canals, the model applied in Empuriabrava.

The wide beach of Empuriabrava

Castelló d'Empúries

Capital of the county of Empúries – nucleus of regional power in the middle ages –, Castelló perfectly preserves traces of its ancient splendour. The church of Santa Maria, justifiably considered to be the Empordà cathedral, seems to-day to be excessive for a population of two thousand inhabitants. However, it draws a significance from a historical perspective. This church has a superb gothic porch with carved figures of the twelve apostles. Next to it is the bell tower, a vestige of the Romanesque temple erected there in the dawn of the second millennium. The church has three naves in which there are chapels, altarpieces and the sepulchres of counts Malgaulí and Hug. Castelló also has a harmonious urban link, the town hall, formerly the fish market, the parish museum and the "Casa Gran", an elegant example of civic gothic.

The church of Santa Maria,
"The Empordà cathedral"

"La Farinera", converted into an
eco-museum

Peralada

The history of Peralada goes back to the dawn of the second millennium when it headed its own county. Known for its wines and sparkling wines, Peralada surprises the visitor because of the integrity and harmony of its preserved medieval collection of buildings. When visiting, it is essential to stop and take in the Romanesque cloister of the convent of Sant Domènec, the gothic cloister of the Carme and that of the church of Sant Martí, where both styles are mixed. Peralada has also conserved several stately mansions that are signs of the social prestige of the town in former times. Amongst these, the castle of Peralada stands out and it is in a perfect state of repair. A large part of its outbuildings now house a Casino. Every summer its gardens are the scene of one of the most ambitious theatre and music festivals in Catalonia.

The castle, home to the casino and summer festivals

Cloister of Sant Domènec

Vilabertran

Vilabertran is a small town situated north of Figueres. It enjoys
a well-deserved fame for its collegiate church of Santa Maria,
an impressive collection of historic buildings in which different
architectural styles are superimposed with unusual elegance and
equilibrium. The buildings were extended here from their start in
the 10th century up to the 19th century. This collection of buildings,
built on a promontory on the orders of the Augustinans, stand
out because of a beautiful Romanesque church whose apses are
a model for proportion and grace. The cloister, in the same style,
is also outstanding. Around the church there are other buildings
that complete this historic collection, such as military fortifications
and various civilian outbuildings in which one can track the
evolution of daily life over the centuries. The historic collection of
buildings, damaged in bellicose incidents, has been duly restored.

*The monument stands on
a promontory*

Detail of the cloister

Sant Llorenç de la Muga

Very closed to the border with France and situated at the foot of
the Pyrenees, Sant Llorenç de la Muga is a quiet, peaceful place in
a collection of medieval buildings. Upon arrival outside the walls,
the visitor comes across the ruins of the local castle that was first
documented in the 13th century. In the urban enclosure, which
is accessed by a portcullis there is the outstanding church of Sant
Llorenç (12th century) that has defensive elements and an imposing
square tower. Fortification architecture is constant in this locality
as evidenced by stretches of ramparts, some battlements and the
different inner and outer towers, like the watchtower that rises
on a hillock on the other side of the Muga. Sant Llorenç attracts
hunters and anglers and it is also an excellent departure point for
excursions to the mountains.

*Stone architecture typical of
the mountains*

*The Canigó from the
Alt Empordà*

*Access via a portcullis to
the medieval enclosure*

Aigüamolls de l'Empordà

Sometimes, dreams become reality. For over a quarter of a century a group of young ecologists has been fighting (with uncertain prospects) to achieve protection status for the Aiguamolls de l'Empordà. This is a unique wetland area where hundreds of animal species dwell or visit seasonally. Today, thanks to a law passed in 1983, the Aiguamolls de l'Empordà Nature Reserve is the second most important destination in Catalonia for bird-watchers. There is a total area of 4,783.5 ha. – 867.5 of these are considered to be a total nature reserve – protected as a result of the diversity of bird life (storks, herons, flamingos, ducks, kites, eagles, falcons, etc.). El Parc, that stretches from Roses to Sant Pere Pescador, is divided into three zones that reflect many other natural habitats.

The fauna enjoys the park's environment

The wetlands of the Estany de Vilaüt

Sant Pere Pescador

Sant Pere Pescador, situated two kilometres from the sea in the centre of the gulf of Roses, organizes its life around both banks of the river Fluvià: the old centre on the left and the marina and urbanization of Llona on the right. A farming and livestock community, Sant Pere Pescador pays careful attention to tourism, especially in the various campsites around the long local beach. This beach stretches from Sant Martí d'Empúries to the mouth of the river Fluvià. It is an ideal spot for windsurfing, as confirmed by the numerous surfers during the violent Tramontana wind. In the last section of the river, that houses corners of languid beauty, such as the Caramany island, water-skiing is practised all year round.

The Caramany island, in a meander of the Fluvià river

Dusk tinges the sky and reflects in the river

Empúries

The Empúries ruins, just a few metres away from the sea, bring together Greek, Iberian and Roman remains. A colony of Greeks from Focea was established in the 5th century B.C. and it was the first settlement in Empúries, known as Paleòpolis. The same group latter founded Neàpolis, that today is a much admired archaeological site. Later, Iberian groups settled here and from 218 B.C. Roman troops set up a camp that over the years transformed itself into a base for the colonization of Hispania. The site, that has been excavated since the beginning of the 20th century, has unearthed the urban net-work of Empúries. Walls, buildings, sculptures, mosaics, jetties and a lot of implements have been unearthed. Some of these items are on exhibit in the museum that complements this first class archaeological site.

"Ambulacrum" in the forum of the Roman city →→

Roman mosaic

Aerial view of the archaeological site

L'Escala

L'Escala, originally a humble fishing neighbourhood in the extreme south of the gulf of Roses, is today an extensive town whose zone of influence stretches from Cala Montgó (in the south) to Sant Martí d'Empúries (in the north).

L'Escala's old quarter was built around the beach of Barques and is flanked by d'en Perris beach. This town centre has a wide range of hotels and shops. There still exist the picturesque and typical anchovy salting stores. The town centre has grown in all directions and especially on the sea-front.

The wooded mountain of Montgó is a good example of this growth. Today it is covered by various urbanizations that are connected with those that surround the port of la Clota, where the local fishing fleet moors. (This building density strongly contrasts however, with the nearby rugged and very tall cliffs that stretch to the south of Montgó, with their incredible views of the Punta del Milà, on the route to L'Estartit). It is a site of great beauty that preserves its natural charm. Going north from la Clota, one reaches the large beach of Riells. El Codolar, with its long promenade, joins Riells with its old town-centre.

North of L'Escala there is one of the most beautiful promenades on the Costa Brava, whose length of some two kilometres attracts walkers, cyclists and skaters. Shaded by tall pines – often beaten by the wind or buried in unstable sand dunes in which they lay down roots – this promenade winds its way along on a characteristic carpet of reddish asphalt among aromas of resin and salt from the sea. On one side are the beaches – Rec, Portitxol, Convent, Sant Martí – and the ruins of

Beaches of Sant Martí d'Empúries

the Greek jetty. On the other side, there is a very old pleasant hotel, the ruins of Empúries, farmed fields flanked by pines and cypresses and on a hillock, the beautiful medieval walled enclosure of Sant Martí d'Empúries, with its ancient buildings arranged around a square that houses the beautiful and sober church and two busy terraces that come to life in the months of fair weather.

This walk from L'Escala to Sant Martí allows the visitor to take in the landscape or, in other words, the essence of a landscape that dazzled, over two thousand years ago, the Greek sailors who established the colony of Empúries.

Terrace opposite the
En Perris beach

Pines at El Pedrigolet

Salted anchovies from L'Escala

Transparent waters in Cala Montgó →

The Dalí route

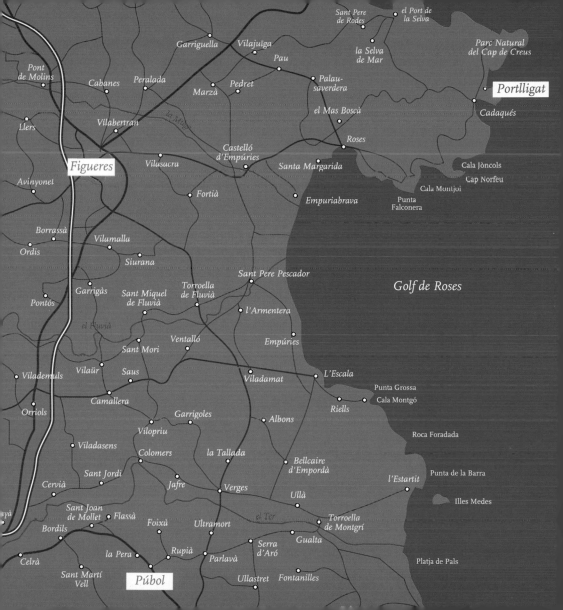

Portlligat

Portlligat, a bare bay north of Cadaqués, is a Dalí landscape par excellence: there are slate coastlines covered by wind resistant thickets facing an electrifying blue sea. It was here that Dalí installed himself in 1930, occupying a simple fisherman's hut. Here he painted numerous canvases, immortalizing his most be loved landscapes. Portlligat was the true home of Dalí who frequented Paris and New York but enjoyed the spring and summer in this corner of the Mediterranean. Other huts were added to the old hut, which was next to an olive grove, and an enclave was formed. Part of it was the house, part of it a studio and part of it was where Dalí held court and received journalists and visitors. Capriciously decorated, Dalí's house was, according to the landmark of the route, opened to the public in 1997, though due to its characteristics, only small groups are admitted by prior notice.

Dalí built his house from old fishing huts

The dovecoat crowned by an enormous egg

Inner patio of the Casa-Museu
A view of the garden and the bay →

Figueres

Figueres, capital of Alt Empordà as well as the Tramontana – the dry and tenacious north wind that sweeps across the area – is a remarkable commercial, gastronomic (the dining rooms of the Motel Empordà are highly recommended) and cultural centre that has some singularly good features in its urban part. Outstanding amongst these is the Museu del Joguet with its collection of historic toys that attracts both children and grown ups equally, the Museu de l'Empordà and especially the Teatre Museu Dalí which is at the head of the Dalí route and is an authentic mass phenomenon on the Spanish museum map. Salvador Dalí was its most famous son but it is also the birthplace of Narcís Monturiol, forefather of the submarine. The church of Sant Pere and the castle of Sant Ferran are amongst its main monuments, although the most characteristic urban space is the wide Rambla, the epicentre of local life.

The Teatre-Museu Dalí, with around a million annual visitors, is the second most visited museum in the Spanish state. It is also a unique cultural centre that brings together an important collection of works of the surrealist painter and is in itself a rare work of art. At the beginning of the 1960's, Dalí started to nurture the idea of building a museum in his town and in this regard he chose the building of the local theatre that was built in the 19th century and was in ruins since 1939, the year the Spanish civil war ended. The choice of this building was, in Dalí's words, due to three facts: "I am a theatrical painter, I was baptized in the church opposite the theatre and it was in the foyer of this theatre that I held my first exhibition". On the ruins

Torre Galatea is also crowned by enormous eggs

Dalí considered himself a "theatrical painter"

of the theatre, enclosed by a reticular transparent dome, the painter designed a museum that opened to the public in September 1974. This complex houses some four thousand works, 1500 of which are on show. They include paintings, sculptures, engravings, holograms, photographs and a remarkable collection of Dalí jewellery that was his last addition to the museum. Together with these works are the spaces and works expressly designed by the painter, such as the Mae West room that reproduces three dimensional "trompe l'oeil" that Dalí was very fond of. There is also a Cadillac parked in the patio of the museum, (the stalls of the old theatre) in whose interior it rains eternally. The collection of works in the museum is completed by artists valued, for one reason or another, by Dalí, such as El Greco, Bouguereau and Duchamp.

Even though Dalí was a generous and open-handed man all his life (his generosity led to him giving away many of his

works), the Teatre-Museu houses a remarkable collection.
The Gala-Salvador Dalí foundation, entrusted to oversee the
functioning of the centre has, over the years, followed a policy
of reinvesting profits by buying art. This has allowed the
enrichment of the wealth of the museum and, in the end, the
opening of additional spaces situated around the Teatre-Museu
where new acquisitions are exhibited.

Dalí's last home was in Torre Galatea, next to the museum.
On his death in 1989, he was buried in a crypt underneath the
museum. It was his wish to lie buried in the heart of the great
artistic creation that he inspired for many years.

*The elements of the
Mae West room*

The bedroom of the Sala Noble
← *The reticular dome and the rainy Cadillac*
Ceiling of the Palau del Vent →→

Púbol

The landscape of Púbol, in the Baix Empordá, 40 kilometres south of Figueres, is very different, almost the opposite to Portlligat, whose rugged coastline is substituted here by a panorama of gentle undulations and farmland. The castle of Púbol, located in the centre of the town of the same name, is the third stage in the Dalí itinerary. This is because, in 1970, Dalí fulfilling an old promise, bought this building – dates from between the 14th and 15th century – for his wife, Gala Diakonova.

Púbol then became a refuge for Gala, a space of her own. It was also the setting for her flings, where Dalí himself was banned from entering without prior notice. The castle of Púbol is a building on three floors, located near the town's church. It has a patio and a French style garden. Dalí and his wife, who bought

The piano-room

The castle and the church

the place in a dilapidated condition, knew how to restore it and preserve its romantic atmosphere but at the same time giving it their particular style. Elephant sculptures, various busts of Wagner as well as Dalí paintings now stand out in the building.

After Gala's death in 1982 and her burial in Púbol, Dalí wanted to be close to his late wife and so installed himself in the castle. His stay there lasted two years when, as a result of a fire in which he suffered serious burns, he was hospitalised and later moved to Figueres. The Casa-Museu Castell Gala Dalí de Púbol has been open to the public since 1996. Here the public can admire ceilings designed by Dalí, the collection of Gala's haute-couture suits and especially to get to know the ambience in which the painter and his wife lived.

One of the "trompe l'oeil" that adorn the house

A detail of the French style garden

Baix Empordà
La Selva

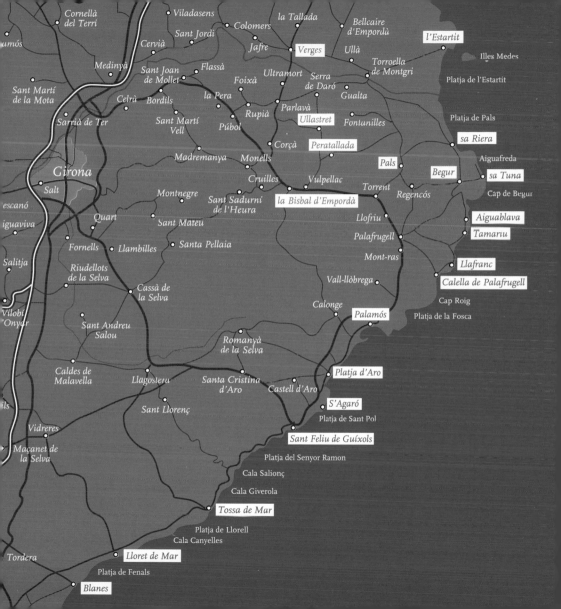

L'Estartit

L'Estartit presents three major special features. It is located opposite the Medes archipelago, made up of seven islets enclaved in one nautical mile of the coast; it spreads out to the shadow of Roca Maura, a severe rocky bulk; and there are kilometres of beaches via which one arrives at the mouth of Ter and Daró as well as the locality of Pals.

L'Estartit has a lot of land behind it. This is a plain that joins it to Torroella de Montgrí, a town that depends on it. L'Estartit has a generous maritime façade. These two factors have conditioned its recent history. The first factor has allowed the building of various urbanizations, hotels, apartment blocks and villas, resulting in L'Estartit becoming a popular holiday destination. The second factor favoured the construction and subsequent enlargements of a spacious marina where old fishing boats, that dominated the jetty thirty years ago, now occupy a residual space in the marina. Also the transformation in 1990 of the Medes zone into a Nature Reserve has turned the archipelago into a dream destination for diving enthusiasts from all over Europe.

The number of daily dives permitted in Medes is around five hundred, and judging by the sea-traffic in the port, this figure is often lower. There are also various glass-bottom boats, that sail in Medes from which one can contemplate the sea bed. All this is possible due to the conservation of the area that has resulted in a spectacular recovery of the flora and, more importantly, the fauna – groupers, conger eels, sea bass, red mullets, white breams, etc. – that live in the Medes waters. One must not forget its dry land where in olden days pirates lived. Today, hundreds of pairs of

The port with the silhouette of El Molinet

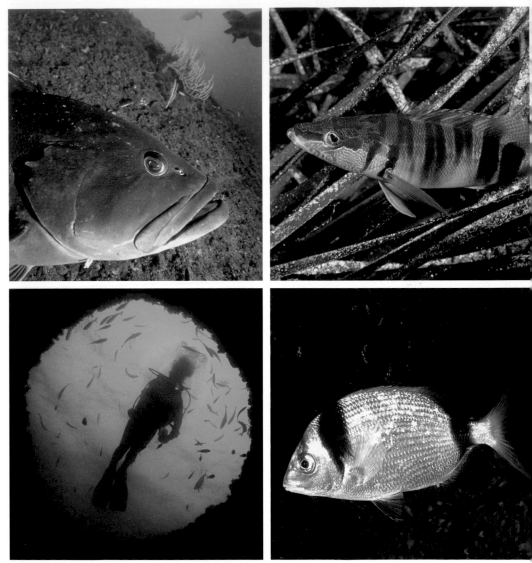

seagulls nest there. A visit to these islands is a must, as is sailing towards the north from the Molinet point and the incredible cliffs that rise from the shore to the navigable tunnel of La Foradada.

All this coastal ruggedness stems from (like the Medes islands) the Montgrí massif that has its most characteristic elevation in Torroella. This is a town with important medieval architectural ruins, an extraordinary summer music festival and a contemporary art collection. The mountain is crowned by the Montgrí castle, erected between the 13th and 14th centuries. Its imposing battlement walls have been restored and are well worth visiting.

*Divers can admire
a varied fauna*

*Aerial view of the Medes
archipelago →→*

*The Platja Gran beach and
the Medes islets*

Pals

The town of Pals, formerly famous for its paddy fields, presents
three different centres. One is its location at the foot of the road
that links Torroella de Montgrí with Begur. Another is its
maritime façade, beyond the Masos de Pals, with its long beach,
its urbanizations, its campsites and its golf-courses. The third is
the medieval quarter of Pedró, built on the hill that dominates
Pals. This enclosure, around the gothic church of Sant Pere, was
carefully restored. It is outstanding for its architecture and
especially for its 360 degree panoramic view. The writer Josep Pla
would take his guests to Pedró in order to show them the wealth
and variety of his land that has a landscape that includes the
Pyrenean range, the Baix Empordà farmlands as well as a vast
portion of sea dominated by the Medes islands.

*El Pedró on the hill over-
looking Pals*

Detail of the mediaeval quarter

One of the roads that ascend to Pedró

← The Torre de les Hores tower over the historic centre

Peratallada

The rock on which this town is located had to be excavated in order to build houses and walls. The name Peratallada, in fact, comes from *pedra tallada* which means cut stone. The old town centre has a distinctly medieval air about it and it is dominated by Peratallada castle and its walled enclosure. Within the enclosure there are various towers of which one stands out for its size and presence which has a quadrangular base. The town also has a beautiful porticoed square whose remaining buildings preserve the flavour of the period. Outside of the Peratallada enclosure, one finds the Romanesque church of Sant Esteve. In the surrounding areas there are other enclaves, equally peaceful, where agriculture is predominant and alien to the activities of the coastline: Vulpellac, Sant Feliu de Boada, Sant Julià, Palau-Sator...

Entrance to the porticoed square

The castle overlooks the walled town

Ullastret

Ullastret has a beautiful medieval quarter (with ruins of ramparts whose structure is perfectly visible and is highlighted even more after an urban restoration project (including paving, restoration of public spaces, lighting, etc.) that was carried out with modern and respectful criteria. It also has interesting elements such as the Romanesque church of Sant Pere and the Plaça de la Llotja. However, the most renowned attraction of Ullastret is its Iberian settlement built towards the 5th century B.C. by the indigenous population, almost at the same time as the Greeks founded Empúries. The settlement was discovered in 1948 in the environs of Ullastret, on the hill of Sant Andreu, and excavated over the following years. It revealed itself to be one of the main archaeological sites of that era for the quality and complexity of its remains.

*View from the mirador
of the settlement →→*

*Remains of the
Iberian settlement*

*The site is of great
Archaeological value*

La Bisbal

After Girona and Figueres, la Bisbal is the main town situated at the "rearguard" of the Costa Brava. The road that goes through it that is often congested is a very long showcase for the local ceramic industry. Kitchen implements, tiles, flowerpots and tubs – coloured in typical blue, green and yellow – are displayed along the busy pavements crowded with both national and foreign buyers. Rich in agriculture – cereals, wine, oil – and livestock farming, La Bisbal preserves in its town centre architectural elements that are worth a mention. Without a doubt, the main one is the castle/palace of the bishops of Girona that houses the region's historical archives. The *voltes* (arcades) of the central artery of the town and the baroque church of Santa Maria (opposite which there is the Bisbal street market) are also buildings of interest.

A potter at his wheel

A global view of the town

Verges

On the night of Maundy Thursday to Good Friday thousands of people occupy the narrow streets of Verges to attend the procession where the "Dance of Death" is performed. This ritual is medieval in origin and mixes religion with paganism and the gruesome with the festive atmosphere. The participants in this procession (that includes Roman soldiers and biblical figures) are a group of dancers swathed in leotards on which are drawn human skeletons. They wear skull masks, are armed with scythes and wear death banderols and clocks with inscriptions in Latin that read *tempus fugit*. The dancers or rather the leaping dancers go round the town reminding everyone of the brevity of existence. Verges, whose church of Sant Julià y Santa Bailissa is noteworthy, lives through this disturbing experience year after year.

Death is the main protagonist in the Maundy Thursday procession

Skyline of the town

Begur

The urban area of Begur sits on the foothills of the promontory that crowns its castle, built in the 17th century from the ruins of a feudal building. Begur, a gentle town that preserves all of its traditional flavour, is also the supply location of the small fishing centres that surround Cap Begur: Sa Riera, Aiguafreda, Sa Tuna, Fornells, Aiguablava... Its elevated position affords sensational views over the beach of L'Estartit and the Medes islands (as well as the gulf of Roses on clear days). For years the centre of the extinct coral harvesting, Begur has an enchanting town centre. It also enjoys a quiet and prosperous life thanks to its current activities as well as the heritage of quite a number of *indianos*, emigrants who, on their return from their American adventures, built large houses that give character to the town.

The castle ruins crown the town

The town, the Pals beach and the Medes islets in the background →→

Typical houses of the "indianos"

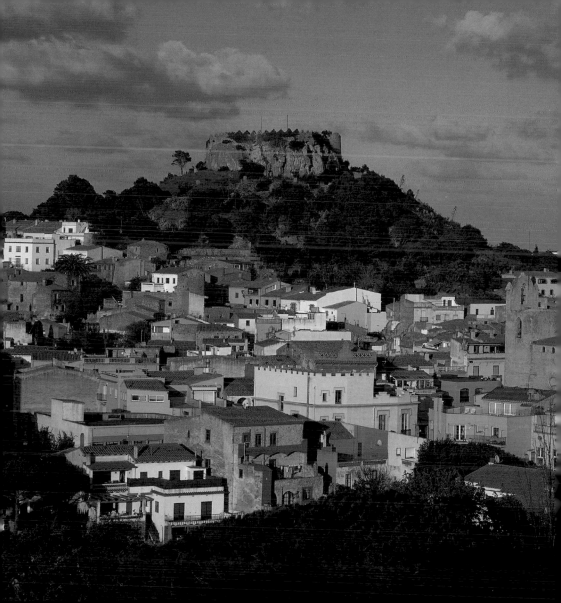

Sa Riera

Sa Riera followed an urban transformation that is very common in this part of the Costa Brava. Originally it was a beach on whose sands fishermen would beach their boats. Small huts and stores to house the fishermen's tools were built next to the beach. The beauty of the coast – covered in pine trees up to the water's edge, which here is an intense blue – motivated the conversion of this collection of huts into second homes that have not fundamentally changed over the passage of time. Generally they are single-family homes, often quite simple, that today occupy the outline of this enclave. Sa Riera faces north to the beach of Pals, before which the nudist beach of Illa Roja is situated, whose access is via a beautiful costal path. A similar path with equally spectacular views connects in a southerly direction with Cap sa Sal.

Illa Roja, on the coast towards Pals

Boats on the beach

Sa Tuna

The magic of Sa Riera is even greater, if that is possible, in
Sa Tuna. Located south of Cap sa Sal and Cala de Aiguafreda,
Sa Tuna warmly welcomes visitors who come by land via a
winding road through pinewoods or by boat, entering its inlet
through the mouth that marks the points of Vaques and Es Plom
The latter is situated at the end of a natural breakwater.
Everything in Sa Tuna breathes seclusion and human scale.
The small size of its sandy beach seems to have immunized it
against the outrageous growth virus that has seriously affected
other locations in the area. On its north coast, Sa Tuna has
buildings literally hanging over the Mediterranean, opposite
which there is a winding road that leads to Aiguafreda. A similar
path in the south leads to the beach of s'Eixugador.

A haven of peace

Aerial view of the cove

Aiguablava

The most characteristic element of Aiguablava today is the
"Parador Nacional de Turismo" (hotel). This is a beautiful and
stylish white building situated, since the 1960's, on the crag of
d'Es Mut point that protects the wonderful beach of Aiguablava.
Owing to its position, it is an ideal place to contemplate the dawn.
It is a heavenly place! So are the nearby coves of Ses Herbes,
Es Tramadiu and the area of the Cabres and Marquesa coves, with
the islets of Cap de Mort and Sa Roncadora. They infinitely
promote the essential features of the Costa Brava. Also heavenly
are Aigua-xellida or Fornells, which in its day was a paradigm of
a little corner far from the madding crowd. This was emphasized
by Josep Pla, perhaps the greatest expert on the area, when he
decided to retire from public life at the end of the Spanish civil war.

From Aiguablava one can walk along the coast to Tamariu.

*Cala Marquesa, north
of Tamariu*

Cala Aigua-xellida →→

*View from Fornells. In the background,
the "Parador Nacional"*

Tamariu

Together with Llafranc and Calella de Palafrugell – separated
by a relatively uninhabited stretch of coast and the Cap of Sant
Sebastiá – Tamariu forms the trio of the large beaches of
Palafrugell (a very active town dedicated to the cork industry,
business and tourism). Tamariu is the smallest of these three
locations and at the same time a very beautiful place. It is known
as a beach but it could also qualify as a cove, taking into account
its size that is on a human scale. Its simple and apt urban layout,
surrounding a tongue of sand among pines and tamarinds makes
it even more enchanting. From Tamariu, the visitor can reach
other very beautiful coves like Pedrosa and Gents, on foot.

*The beach with its habitual
summer atmosphere*

The bay of Tamariu

Llafranc

Llafranc closes one of the most rugged areas of the Costa Brava (that starts with the beach of Racó, in Pals, in the north) and it stands out because of its cosy and contained buildings. They turn it into a bustling town in the summer without turning it into a bleak and lifeless place in the winter months. It has a harbour – also quite small – and affords superb views at the top of the lighthouse that is situated on the Cap of Sant Sabastià. From the lighthouse complex, that now houses a hotel and restaurant, one can contemplate the coastline towards the south (Llafranc, Calella, the Forcats point, Cap Roig, Cap de Planes etc.), observe the interior up to Palafrugell, or glance at the blue immensity of the Mediterranean, on a green vertical in which some haughty agaves stand out.

Aerial view with the Sant Sebastià lighthouse in the background

Boats on the beach

Calella de Palafrugell

The white and welcoming porches of Port Bo make up the central enclave of Calella de Palafrugell, which is also one of the most characteristic places on the Costa Brava. It lies opposite the beach and there are boats in the water. Despite its growth, this town has preserved its architectural identity.

In contrast to Tamariu and Llafranc, Calella has more than one beach owing to the reefs along its coastline that divide its sandy areas into various segments. The largest beach is that of Canadell, from where one can set off on a walk to the Calella tower (16th century) and then, following a beautiful coastal path, one reaches Llafranc. In the surrounding area of the beach of Port Bo (which despite its limited size attracts tens of thousands of people every year in July for the traditional habaneras festival), there are the beaches of Port Pelegrí, Sota Can Calau, Port de Malaespina and Sota de Sant Genís.

South of Calella – and up to Cala de la Fosca, which is already in the Palamós area – there is one of the largest areas of the Costa Brava still unspoilt by urban occupation. A dirt path that goes through the wooded mass that covers this bit of virgin coast, provides the only access to enchanted spots like the botanical gardens of Cap Roig and, on the shore, Golfet, Cala Massoni, Cala del Vedell, Cala el Crit, Cala Font Morisca, Cala Pomes... This is a stretch of coastline that is ideal for sailing and diving.

The beaches of Can Calau,
Port Bo and Malaespina

Characteristic porches of houses by the sea
← Cala el Golfet, south of Calella
The traditional "cantada d'havaneres" festival attracts multitudes →→

Palamós

Palamós is one of the largest port towns in Catalonia, the third largest after Barcelona and Tarragona even though its population is much lower than the other two cities. Its old quarter is built on a wide projection that ends at the Molí point where the Palamós lighthouse is situated. At the south and the north of this projection, the town of Palamós located its two ports. On one side there is the commercial and fishing port (where the very bustling daily fish market auctions take place in the small hours of the fish caught the previous night by the powerful local fishing fleet) and on the other side there are boats moored in the marina.

Palamós has grown in an orderly fashion in all directions. Towards the south, along the beach of playa Gran, there is the larger stretch of the town, and the interior front part towards La Bisbal up to the north.

Given its historical traditions (it was one of the medieval Catalonian bases for the Mediterranean expansion to Italy and Greece), its central location in the Costa Brava and its various activities, Palamós has offered, since olden times, all types of services. Amongst its attractions is the gothic church of Santa Maria del Mar, the Cau de la Costa Brava Museum (with interesting collections of paintings, coins, shells, etc.). Its Sunday open-air market is also remarkable, being one of the most colourful and lively in the region.

As well as this urban profile, Palamós has known how to conserve (and continues to do so with ecologists) coastal stretches that maintain the integrity, purity and flavour of long ago. This begins to be evident starting from La Fosca (to the North

of Cap Gros), a long beach that is divided by the so-called
La Fosca rock that is a traditional summer enclave for families
from Palamós and Gerona. Going beyond Sant Esteve point in
a northerly direction, one reaches Cala S'Alguer which is a
delightful car-free spot where the old fishermen's huts have
been converted, with few changes, into second homes. Then,
following the coastal path, one reaches Cala Castell, a wide sandy
area with no buildings. This is a significant exception in the area
and is the reason for a long dispute between conservationists
and property developers (to date resolved in favour of the
former). Going round La Corbetera point, other marvellous coves
await the visitor. These are accessible on foot and have pines
growing between rocks that kiss the sea and include la Sania,
Els Canyers, Estreta and others.

Cala Els Canyers

*The Christmas Race sets sail
in Palamós harbour* →→

Cala s'Alguer

Platja d'Aro

After leaving Palamós and Sant Antoni de Calonge behind, one reaches Platja d'Aro, the next large coastal town. As in other enclaves located next to a beach of exceptional size, Platja d'Aro went from being a tiny, almost non-existing settlement at the beginning of the 20th century, to a disproportionate collection of tall hotels and apartment buildings that today cast a shadow, even at inappropriate times of the day, over its fine sands.

Like Lloret de Mar, Platja d'Aro has a Las Vegas feel about it: a giant complex dedicated to leisure. In this case it is not gambling, merely holiday-making. It has an incredible network of services. Spectacular illuminated signs and advertising slogans of all kinds that mark out the wide main avenue are evidence of this.

Crowds were not always the distinctive sign of Platja d'Aro. The long stretch of sand (two kilometres) of Platja d'Aro, that today is a focal point for mass tourism, is paradoxically situated very close to Cap Roig – a crag with intrepid pines that enters the sea. It is joined to dry-land by a small sandy isthmus. This place represents a paradigm of what were the best spots of the Costa Brava: a meeting point for the land and the sea, discreet and reserved that, notwithstanding certain buildings, still preserves today an atmosphere that for around a century attracted the first foreign holidaymakers. When the visitor strolls through the area, the reasons for this attraction are perfectly understandable.

All the coastal strip that stretches from Torre Valentina (bordering on the beach of Sant Antoni de Calonge) to the Cavall Bernat rock (already touching the playa Gran beach of

Platja d'Aro) reflects the best and most characteristic attributes of the Costa Brava: rocky terrain and covered in pines that descend towards the sea in abrupt circumstances.

In this area, that can be totally walked around on a spectacular coastal road, there are some hidden spots of unusual beauty that are not always easy to reach where buildings have been built with a certain touch. In this regard, it is worth mentioning the beaches of Treumal, Cap Roig, Bella Dona, Canyers, d'en Ros, Sa Cova...

On the other side of Platja Gran beach, beyond the Port d'Aro marina (that offers an unusual interior model of a marina), there is Cala de Sa Conca which is outstanding for its size.

Cala del Pi

Cap Roig beach with the crag that gives it its name

S'Agaró

S'Agaró started to take shape in the 1920's with the aim of high-level urbanization located in a certainly privileged spot of the Costa Brava. Highly reputed architects of the time – Masó, Florensa, Folguera – were commissioned to plan buildings in S'Agaró that often highlight the serenity and elegance of *Noucentisme*. Apart from its legendary hotel – La Gavina –, its splendid houses, numerous services, viewpoints and balustrades, S'Agaró also has a successful plan of general landscaping. Lastly, it is again worth mentioning the beautiful coastal road above the sea that is carefully thought out and stretches from the En Pau point (close to the beach of Sant Pol with its characteristic early 20th century villas) to the spacious cove of Sa Conca.

Modernist villa on the beach of Sant Pol

S'Agaró and, in the background, the beach of Sant Pol

Sant Feliu de Guíxols

Sant Feliu de Guíxols is one of the oldest urban centres of the Costa Brava. The cork industry and sea traffic laid the foundations for its growth process, especially in the 20th century. Tourism, in the last fifty years, has supplemented the prosperity of the town.

Sant Feliu extends in an orderly arrangement towards the interior. However, its façade is maritime and it stretches in front of the beach and its yacht club and harbour, whose breakwater almost closes the bay completely. The chapel of Sant Elm, on the mound of the same name, affords a beautiful panoramic view of the Mediterranean and wide views on Sant Feliu. The town joins together distinct architectural elements of interest. The main element is probably the Benedictine monastery of Sant Feliu of which the highlight is the pre-Romanesque portico of Porta Ferrada. Also outstanding are the modern municipal theatre and the picturesque buildings of the early 20th century situated on the promenade. Amongst these is the "Nuevo Casino La Constancia" that is Arabic in style and ochre in colour.

Towards the direction of Santa Cristina de Aro, one finds Pedra Alta, a spectacular oscillating rock. Also worth attention in the surrounding area is the tough route of some 25 kilometres that reaches Tossa. This is a conceptual compendium of the Costa Brava: revered, exhausting and jealous of its countless and marvellous secret spots.

Sant Feliu, seen from the south

The curious building of the Nuevo Casino La Constancia
Pine trees grow to the very edge of the cliffs →
Reefs keep sailors at bay →→

Tossa de Mar

Tossa de Mar offers one of the most characteristic outlines of the Costa Brava thanks, basically, to its old town (which is encircled by battlement walls) that sits proudly above Cap de Tossa. The walls date from the 12th century and the houses protected by them were mostly built starting from the 15th century. Despite their venerable age and the beating sea and wind, the three large cylindrical towers and other smaller ones that give identity to the complex are in a very good state of preservation.

Just by arriving in Tossa, the visitor feels inevitably captivated by this old town that is in a constant and loving process of restoration. The peaceful and steep streets that cross it, often refreshed by the abundance of flowers in pots and flower beds or climbing up aged stone walls, or beside carved wooden front doors, afford endless visual enjoyment.

The town centre, sitting on a hillside that faces north, has an agreeable feel and is without doubt responsible for the attraction that Tossa has had historically – even before the boom of the Costa Brava – on a legion of painters and artists who, like Marc Chagall and Yves Klein, frequented it and opened studios there. The municipal museum, located within the Batlle palace, a gothic building in the old town, is testimony to the presence in the town of many of those artists.

From the walls of the Vila Vella (the old town), where, at its highest point, there are ruins of a 15th century gothic temple, one has splendid views of Tossa in addition to a promise of countless treasures on the north coast. Also and in particular one can admire fully from the top Vila Nova that grew outside the walls and that today houses most hotels and services that were set up by the city to accommodate its ever increasing number of visitors.

Situated behind the beach of Tossa (Platja Gran), on whose sands Ava Gardner frolicked during the filming of "Pandora and the flying Dutchman", Vila Nova has known how to grow with discretion without losing its local character. The beach of Platja Gran is complemented in the north by that of Mar Menuda. From this point starts a series of bends on the road that leads to Sant Feliu. There is not even one merciful stretch of straight road on this road that was mentioned in the previous chapter! Over a distance of 25 kilometres it runs along one of the most beautiful coastal areas of the region. Taking this road on a sunny morning

One of the steep side streets of Vila Vella

Cala es Codolar, beneath the walled enclosure

(or even in winter when one finds it almost deserted) is extraordinarily spectacular. One is faced with a tranquil sea of sparkling liquid silver. Also, going along this road one passes a rosary of surprisingly beautiful and solitary coves largely unknown to the public.

On the road from Tossa to Sant Feliu one can reach, for example, the cove of Pola or the very discreet cove of Giverola where despite its considerable beach, there is no access sign from the road. It is as if everything aspires to preserve its tranquillity. One also comes across the cove of Futadera and Salionç where the mix of oaks and pines announces the change in the region. Further up there is the long and narrow stretch of sand of the beach of Señor Ramón. There are also those of Canyerets and the cove of Joana. One must not forget, even though one is on another route, the beaches located south of Tossa, some of which are beautiful such as Llorell.

The beach of Llorell
The beach of Mar Menuda →
The beach of Tossa and the Vila Vella →→

Lloret de Mar

This town represents one of the main tourist-urban phenomena of the Costa Brava. Little remains of the old gentle coastal fishing village situated in front of the splendid beach that delimits the Sa Caravera point and Sa Caleta, above which the characteristic castle of En Platja rises. Today the place is one of the most sought-after by tour operators from all over Europe. In a curious process of imitation, urban corners of distinct European union countries (Great Britain, Germany, Holland...) have sprung up to make the tourists' stay in this location more comfortable and familiar. This is how that virgin Lloret of the beginning of the 20th century has changed into a town of diffused architecture and signs written in different languages where every spring and summer hundreds of thousands of tourists pass through hoping to stretch out a few days of enjoyment at more than economic prices.

Lloret has various outstanding urban elements, such as its wide promenade that runs parallel to the beach, flanked by graceful palm trees; the Sant Romà church (outstanding are its gothic main door and altarpiece); the town hall, Isabelline in style and located at the head of the promenade; and the bronze statue of "Dona marinera" that faces the sea and is located on the crag of El Rompent. It is also worth visiting the nearby castle of Sant Joan in Fenals and the chapel of Santa Cristina that rises between the beaches of Santa Cristina and Treumal.

For sure, a very large part of the visitors who choose Lloret as a holiday destination prefer the pubs, discos, bars, flamenco shows, bowling alleys and other establishments in which they

The beach and promenade

A bridge path follows the coastline

can relax, to other attractions. In this respect, Lloret has a wide variety to offer that can be considered inexhaustible. The town also has facilities probably not found together in any other locality on the Costa Brava, such as its casino, a bull-ring and on the Vidreres road, a splendid water park.

The spot on which Lloret stands was, prior to its huge transformation, a place of great beauty and charm. To a certain extent it still is and this is evident by going to the spacious and, in places, beautiful stretches of the coast that surround this cosmopolitan town. South of Lloret one can visit coves such as Treumal and Santa Cristina. One can also visit the beach of Boadella and the En Serrahima cove. Between these two and before that of Fenals, there are the gardens of Santa Clotilde, a beautiful, quiet place close to the mansion of the same name.

In the north, the beauty of the coast is more abundant. Firstly one finds the coves of Els Frares and d'en Trons, that provide the first dose of peace amongst the overcrowding that reigns on the large beach of Lloret. Then, further along, after the Cabdells point, there are spaces such as the Tortuga cove, the spacious cove of Canyelles (this has a small marina), the Morisca cove, the beaches of Porto Pi, Lorell, Carles and Llevador.

The beach of Sa Caleta and Lloret castle

The palm lined promenade
The cove of Canyelles is one of the most appreciated →

Blanes

The Costa Brava, an abrupt rocky succession that stretches to the French border, gives to Blanes its last or, if one prefers, first death throes. The lithic outline of the landscape diminishes, reaching the Palomera point, the last expression of a coastal orography that in the nearby province of Maresme (further south) levels out definitively. A fishing village with a great coastal trade tradition during the 19th century, Blanes has a beautiful semicircular bay, closed in the north by a square shaped harbour. It has a gentle promenade shaded by pine trees and plane trees. From the ruins of the castle of Sant Joan there is a serene view of the town. On the same promontory one can visit the botanical gardens of Mar i Murtra. At the foot of these gardens, in a northerly direction, there are the coves of Forcanera and Sant Francesc.

Cala de Sant Francesc, north of Blanes →→

The panorama from the castle of Sant Joan

Mar i Murtra botanical gardens

Girona
Pla de l'Estany
La Garrotxa

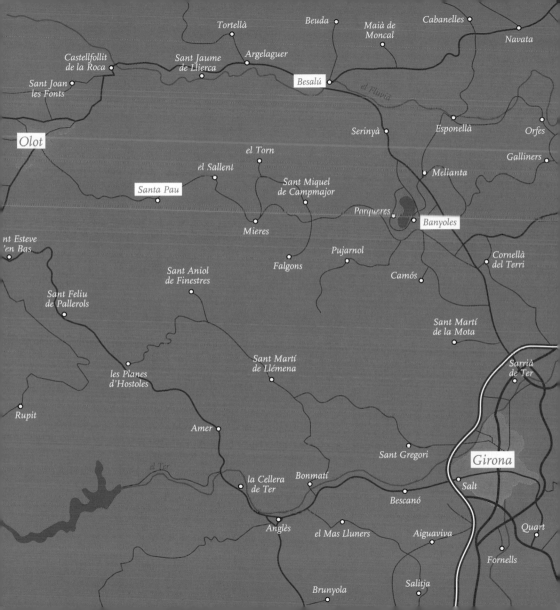

Girona

The rivers Ter and Onyar – whose urban façade of its banks has been repainted with Florentine tones – converge in Girona, one of the four main Catalonian cities. There is an historical undertone of discretion, economic prosperity and military gestures.

Girona is a city of monuments that has in its imposing cathedral (accessible via a no less majestic flight of steps) its most characteristic treasures. It has a Romanesque cloister, a gothic nave and a baroque façade. The cathedral houses the tomb of Ramon Berenguer II and the Charlemagne throne as well as the Tapís de la Creació (the tapestry of the Creation), a fabulous work that has been splendidly preserved.

The Onyar and the town centre, overlooked by the cathedral

A rainy and satisfied city with a great history, Girona has experienced a revitalizing and invigorating transformation in the

Autumn dusk in the Devesa

past twenty years. One of the axis for change has been the strengthening of its university, that has been transformed into a centre for not only economic but also social and urbanistic development. The section of the old walls that has been carefully restored around the university buildings and located in the high part of the city, affords a priceless viewpoint over Girona. Adjacent to the university buildings is the restored *Call jueu* (jewish quarter). This is a nucleus of steep small streets around La Força street and the "Isaac el Cec" building, that has become a yearned for tourist destination for the international Jewish community.

In Girona it is also worth visiting the splendid monastery of Sant Pere de Galligants – seat of the Archaeological Museum –, Sant Nicolau and Sant Feliu, the Arab baths, the city museum and the Devesa, the large and gentle grove that is a favourite walk for people from Girona.

Gardens on the banks of the Ter

Pujada de Sant Domènec,
in the old town

The cathedral houses the magnificent Tapís de la Creació

The access steps enhance the Seu complex →

Inside the Arab baths

← *A typical narrow street in the old town centre*

The colourful façades are reflected in Onyar →→

Banyoles

Catalonia has various lakes. However, its "lake city" par excellence is Banyoles. With a surface area that is a third of that of Banyoles and a six kilometre perimeter – ideal for walks or cycling –, *l'estany* determines the landscape and part of the town's activity. Mists turn it into a magical scene. Its two kilometre length make it an ideal place for rowing, a sport with a long tradition in Banyoles. It was chosen as a secondary venue in the 1992 Olympic Games. A thousand-year-old city, Banyoles has beautiful buildings like the monastery of Sant Esteve (neoclassic on gothic remains) and the Plaça Mayor which is porticoed. Some of its buildings date from the 12th century. Visiting the archaeological museum, one comes across the "Banyoles jaw", the oldest remains of a Catalonian!

Recreational boats plying the waters of "l'estany"

A romantic view of the lake

Besalú

The medieval complex of Besalú, splendidly preserved, offers
an historic counterpoint to the landscape of the Costa Brava.
Amongst the different architectural elements of Besalú, a fortified
11th century Romanesque bridge stands out. It is an imposing
curved construction whose arches plant their pillars above the
river Fluvià. From this bridge – visible upon arrival at Besalú and
that can be admired from the Jewish baths of *Mikwà* – one reaches
an urban enclosure that contains the church of Sant Pere which is
a notable attraction. This is an Italianate church with a sober
façade where the figures of two lions stand out. It has an
ambulatory in its apse. Similarly robust is the church of Sant
Vicenç and the porticos of Carrer Tallaferro that lead to the old
Jewish quarter. The solidity of stone presides around Besalú.

Aerial view of the town

*The fortified
Romanesque bridge*

Olot

Olot, capital of the Garrotxa region, is an active industrial and commercial centre. It likes to present itself as the city of volcanoes as it has in its area the cones of up to 38 volcanoes. At a height of over 400 metres above sea-level and in an area of green valleys with the Pyrenees as a backdrop, Olot is equidistant from Girona, Figueres, Ripoll and Vic. This privileged position has stimulated its vigour, favoured its wealth and deep rooted cultural tradition. Together with its architectural heritage–limited due to earthquakes in the 15th century but still with elements of value such as the church of Sant Esteve and the Renaissance cloister of Carme – it has a more than notable museum interest. In this regard a main museum of interest is the "Museu Comarcal de la Garrotxa", the fiefdom of the landscape artists of

The market draws people from all over the region

Relaxing in the fresh air of Parc Nou

the so-called Olot School that made the town famous. There are paintings as well as sculptures by, amongst others, Clarà and Blay and the celebrated oil-painting of "La carga" by Casas.

It is worth mentioning places near Olot that are protected by the Garrotxa Volcanic Nature Reserve which covers 12,000 hectares. Volcanoes such as Montsacopa (that, being in the centre of Olot, allows both the study of its characteristics as well as admiring the town centre) and Croscat are a must to visit. The latter rises next to the Fageda d'en Jordà, an immense and magical beech-wood that the poet Maragall aptly described as a "liberating prison". Within this beech-wood (that is coloured in autumn with a symphony of yellows, greens and browns that illuminate the sun's rays; there is a carpet of fallen leaves, reddish earth and moss) one indeed feels liberated from the world.

The crater of the Santa Margarida volcano

Fageda d'en Jordà, a captivating nature area

Santa Pau

A visit to Olot and Fageda d'en Jordà has its natural limits up to
the medieval enclave of Sant Pau via its gentle, green valley that is
marked out by, among others, the volcanoes of Croscat, Puig de la
Costa, Santa Margarida, Roca Negra, Puig Subià, Simó, etc...
Articulated around its castle, Sant Pau stands out for its Pyrenean-
style architecture that is very noticeable in its main square, the
Plaça Mayor, the seat of the old livestock market, characterized by
a long porticoed stone façade and a series of wooden balconies
below the cornice line. In this square there is also the gothic church
of Santa Maria. The elevated situation of Sant Pau affords a superb
observation point over the surrounding and pleasant volcanic
landscape of the Garrotxa nature reserve. The views are only
cutted by the irregular outline of the Finestres mountain range.

*Façade of one of the
porticoed houses*

Pyrenean style architecture

© *Text*
LLÀTZER MOIX

© *Photographs*
JORDI PUIG *Cover and pages:* 2, 9, 12, 16-17, 20, 21, 22, 23, 25, 26, 27, 29, 30-31, 32, 33, 35, 36-37, 40, 43, 44-45, 47, 49, 50, 51, 52-53, 54, 57, 58, 59, 60, 62, 63, 64, 65, 66-67, 68, 69, 74-75, 80, 81, 84, 86, 88, 90-91, 93, 95, 97, 100, 101, 102, 103, 107, 109, 110-111, 112, 115, 116, 117, 118, 119, 120-121, 122, 123, 124, 125, 126, 127, 128-129, 130, 131, 132, 143, 145, 146-147, 148, 152-153, 159, 160, 162, 164-165, 176, 182-183, 186, 187, 188, 190, 192, 200, 201, 202, 204, 205 *and* 207 ·
JAUME SERRAT 10-11, 15, 24, 34, 41, 42, 48, 56, 71, 85, 114, 136-137, 140, 141, 151, 156, 158, 170 *and* 181 ·
RICARD PLA 70, 79, 87, 157, 168, 171, 172-173, 179, 180, 194-195 *and* 198 · **JOAN MARC LINARES** 46, 77, 138 *and* 166 ·
JORDI TODÓ 55, 73, 113 *and* 203 · **CARLES VIRGILI** 108 (4) · **QUIM TOR** 133, 134 *and* 139 ·
JOSEP FERRER 144, 150 *and* 163 · **JOAN OLIVA** 175, 177 *and* 178 · **MIGUEL RAURICH** 61 *and* 196 ·
ORIOL MASPONS / FUNDACIÓ GALA-SALVADOR DALÍ 89 *and* 94 · **J. PUIG-PERE VIVAS** 191 *and* 193 ·
MIQUEL FLYNN 28 · **ALBERT HERAS** 72 · **NEIL PEACHEY** 78 · **TORNER / FUNDACIÓ GALA-SALVADOR DALÍ** 96 ·
SALVADOR DALÍ, FUNDACIÓ GALA-SALVADOR DALÍ / VEGAP, Barcelona, 2003 *Foto* **TORNER** 98-99 ·
RICARD CARRERAS 135 · **ÁNGEL GAGO** 169 · **RAMON MANENT** 189 · **TINO SORIANO** 197 ·
BRIANSÓ-CASTELLS 198 ·

Graphic design
MARTÍ ABRIL

Graphic edition
JORDI PUIG

Translation
NICHOLAS NABOKOV

Photomecanics
TECNOART

Printed by
INDEX
05-2007

Legally reg. **B-16379-2007**

ISBN **978-84-8478-018-2**

TRIANGLE POSTALS
Sant Lluís, Menorca
Tel. 971 15 04 51
Fax 971 15 18 36
e-mail: triangle@infotelecom.es